AF576417

DECORATION AND ITS USES

DECORATION AND ITS USES

BY EDWARD JOHNSTON

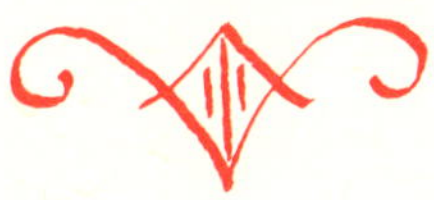

Transcribed by John Ch. Tarr from The Imprint, 1913

A Double Elephant Press Book

TEN SPEED PRESS

TEN SPEED PRESS
P.O. Box 7123
Berkeley, California 94707

Cover calligraphy by Christopher Stinehour

Library of Congress Cataloging-in-Publication Data

Johnston, Edward, 1872–1944.
Decoration and its uses / Edward Johnston ; handwritten by John C. Tarr.
p. cm.
ISBN 0-89815-401-4
1. Calligraphy. 2. Penmanship. I. Tarr, John Charles.
II. Title.
Z43.J775 1991
745.6′1—dc20 90-49400
CIP

First hardcover edition, 1991

Printed in the United States of America

1 2 3 4 5 - 95 94 93 92 91

Introduction

EDWARD JOHNSTON (1872-1944), it has been said, probably brought more genius to a single handicraft than any craftsman who ever lived yet he was practically unknown to the general public.

Perhaps his ancestry (Elizabeth Fry, the prison reformer was his great-great aunt) accounted for much of his character. Devoutly religious, he demonstrated an infinitely patient & avid search for perfection in his craft in spite of his consistently poor health. The latter & his indifference to commercial success restricted the work that he was able to undertake.

Johnston became interested in calligraphy early in life. He went to Edinburgh to study medicine but his own ill health forced him to abandon his studies. The sympathetic encouragement of his uncle who was a successful business man, enabled him to pursue his extraordinary bent towards letter-forms.

A small private income was certainly no hindrance. He profited by his studies of manuscripts in the British Museum and developed his own intuitive gift to the mastery of his chosen craft. Contact with W.R. Lethaby who inspired, by means of the Arts & Crafts Movement, Ruskin & Morris, had considerable influence on his teaching at the London Central School of Arts & Crafts, where he began to teach in 1899, under Lethaby and later, in 1904, at the Royal College of Art.

Johnston's distinguished pupils include Eric Gill, the calligrapher, wood-engraver, sculptor & type-designer, Percy Smith of the Dorian Studio, and Graily Hewitt, his successor at the Central School, whom he inspired with his own driving enthusiasm.

His work had a tremendous impact on German calligraphers, notably Anna Simons and Rudolf Koch who, practising the teaching of Johnston & Gill, dominated the whole of German type design.

Apart from his somewhat limited production of illuminated addresses, Johnston worked for the Doves Press of Cobden-Sanderson & Emery Walker for whom he designed initial letters and also for Count Kessler's Cranach Presse.

In 1906 he published his classic manual, "Writing and

Illuminating and Lettering," a manual of uniquely clear and practical exposition and instruction which is still the Bible of present-day calligraphers and illuminators.

In the middle of World War I, he designed the famous san-serif for the London Underground. This clear legible letter, based on the classic Roman capitals of the Trajan column in the forum in Rome, still informs Londoners in their metropolis although few know the name of Johnston. Like his famous compatriot, Sir Christopher Wren, Johnston might well have said (as to the visitor of St. Paul's cathedral), "si monumentum requiris, circumspice."

The late Beatrice Warde became interested in lettering and typography as a professional through reading Johnston's manual. Sir Francis Meynell of the Nonesuch Press acclaims Johnston as "one of the greatest men of my time". In Johnston's rubrication of a small book printed by Sir Francis in 1918, he said, "When I want a reminder that there can be loveliness in the quickening line of something austere & formal, I look with wonder and delight on these initials."

Johnston's essential influence was artistic rather

than practical. He sought to make lettering an artistic craft and, not without risking archaism, recalled the Tours ninth-century minuscule hands. Thus he broke with the humanistic tradition of the Renaissance chancery cursive and its later developments & modification. His approach was retrogressive but he nevertheless had a profound effect on typography while the current commercial handwriting, as taught in schools, remained untouched.

By the time of World War I at least, Stanley Morison, Beatrice Warde and myself, among others, were using the chancery script as an every day handwriting &, in 1926, Frederic Warde published "The Calligraphic Models of Ludovico degli Arrighi surnamed Vicentino" with an introduction by Morison. About the same time, Alfred Fairbank, a calligrapher of the Johnstonian school, also favoured a reversion in handwriting to the humanistic cursive for those who desired to acquire a good everyday hand. This script, if it can emancipate itself from the use of the semi-looped ascending letters of Arrighi, could be eventually our current handwriting. It is now widely taught in Britain and the U.S.A. In this eventuality the revival may be credited, through Fairbank and others to Edward Johnston, master craftsman, lovable character and - fortunately for all of us - unworldly enough to pursue a vanishing art.

The present edition of this series of articles, written in 1913 in "The Imprint", was transcribed as a student exercise in 1930 by me, a grateful ex-student of Johnston & Graily Hewitt. It is offered less as an example of the "foundational hand" of Johnston than as a valuable but little known exposition of his teaching.

John C. Tarr

DECORATION AND ITS USES

DECORATION AND ITS USES

BY EDWARD JOHNSTON

THESE papers will deal directly with the decoration that is appropriate to book & letters, and, in particular will consider what the modern craftsman may expect to get out of the study or practice of penmanship. But as the principles of decoration, which I hope to discuss here, are in all crafts fundamentally alike, the larger title may be justified.

As the word decoration has become somewhat artificialised, not to say degraded, it is worth recalling its more primitive and exact meaning. I take the following definition from an ordinary standard dictionary (Annadale's Concise, 1899).

Decorate (L. decoro, decoratum, from decus, decor, comeliness, grace; akin decent.) To deck with something becoming or ornamental; to adorn; to beautify; to embellish . . . .

I should like to lay particular stress on the Latin derivation, comeliness and grace, & the kinship with the word decent.

Again, as the word Use is one for which we all have a private interpretation and is therefore apt to be narrowed and ab-used, it is worth refreshing our memories with the wider sense of a dictionary definition. I take the following:

> Use, n. [O. Fr. us, use, from L. *usus*, use, of using; service, need, from *utor, usus*, to use (whence also *utility, utensil . . . abuse*, etc.)] The act of employing anything, or the state of being employed; . . the quality that makes a thing proper for a purpose; . . continued or repeated practice; wont; usage; . . . . .

In this reconsideration of my title I find that there are four meanings that I wish to make clear

(1) The Value of Decoration ["What's the use of it?"]

(2) The Appropriateness of it ["Does it fit?"]

(3 & 4) Its Practice & Usage ["How it's done" and "How it works."].

Later in these papers I hope to develop & meet the first two questions, here I shall deal specially with practice & usage, &, in the discussion of the craft with which I am most familiar, namely penmanship, try to show "how it is done." No man, however well he knows his craft, can tell another "how it is done"; he can show to another by example of his craft, only what that other is able to see, in most cases, a series of unrelated details. No man can know "how it is done" until he himself has done the same thing, & even to that achievement, in its ultimate sense, we can only approach nearer. Let me, therefore, ask the reader who would approach this subject to get or cut for himself a very broad-nibbed pen, made from a quill, or bamboo cane, or a reed, and with that in his hand, to follow the argument practically.

Chapter I. Formal Writing & the Broad-nibbed Pen

BY penmanship I mean more particularly that kind of writing in which a broad-nibbed pen is used to form the letters. It is conveniently referred to by the name of "formal writing," and the early varieties of it are distinguished from the "running hands," or ordinary writing, by being called the "book hands," because for something like two thousand years books were made in such writing, before the invention of printing. In fact, the book as we know it, owes the shapes of its letters and even its familiar form & general plan, not to the printers, but to the early scribes or writers of the formal hands. And it is not too much to hope that modern printers & others who are interested in the production & decoration of books — even if they "cannot do" their writing "in the old way" — may profit by a study of the methods & principles of that penmanship on which their art is founded.

The three most important things about the broad nibbed pen, technically considered, are:

1. That it naturally writes regular thick & thin and graduated strokes, according to its direction (not its pressure)

2. That the character of its writing depends upon the relative width of the nib in proportion to the height & breadth of the writing, and upon

3. The direction (or relation to a horizontal line) of the thin edge of the nib.

And here I may add the reminder that the edge of the nib must be kept true & sharp: a blunt pen has its uses for the skilled writer, but, as a tool in the hand of a student of formal writing, it not only damages or blunts the forms of his letters but hinders or blunts his own apprehension & his constructive faculties.

The fact that a broad-nibbed pen produces thick or thin strokes in absolute relation to its direction, distinguishes it from every other tool & enables it to make, out of collections of simple strokes, letters of marked character & finish with the greatest possible regularity and ease (a). Such

a pen writing

b skeleton forms

c compound

(a) Simple written Formal writing made with a broad-nib
(b) & (c) Simple skeleton & compound forms made with a pointed tool

letters, consisting of collections of simple strokes, may correctly be described as "simple written" forms. Now the simple written letters naturally produced by other tools are generally of the nature of skeleton forms (b), & to make letters with the character & finish that are to be obtained by varying widths of the strokes, the craftsman has to resort to a building-up process, making a number of strokes – or of such scratches, chippings, stitches, cuts, as his styles, chisels, needles, gravers, etc., may naturally make – to form one compound stroke (such letters, in which the thick strokes are compound, may be termed "compound" or "built-up" letters (c). The pointed pen, or brush, it is true, in the hand of a skilled writer can simulate the ease & finish of the broad nib, & give us their own equivalent character – in some sort also a "simple written" letter. The different letter making tools & their virtues, however, will be discussed later: here we are considering the educative value of the broad-nibbed pen for those not specially skilled in writing, as the tool, that, historically speaking, made our letters for us, & is capable of remaking them now.

If our formal writing owes its thick strokes to the broad nib, it follows that the actual width of the nib is of great importance, determining as it does the actual width of our strokes.

"Broad" is, of course, a relative term, and it is the width of our strokes in relation to their height, that we must mainly consider. The relative width of the nib, for instance, chiefly determines the "weight" of a letter, & it is obvious that similar letters of the same height (and breadth) will be "heavy" or "light" accordingly as they are made with a relatively wide or relatively narrow nib.

formal

formal

Examples of heavy & light writing

The width of the nib in this manner not only determines the weight, but also largely controls the actual forms of the letters (as may be seen by a careful examination of the figure opposite), so that their character may, in these respects, be said to depend on it. Naturally, the wider the nib, the more it controls the forms, & the more marked becomes their pen character, while the narrower the nib, the less marked is the pen character of the letters, & the more is their formation left to the writer's choice & skill. If we take, for example the following extreme cases, these differences are at once made apparent. Let us write an o and an n in letters 3/8" high with a nib 1/8" wide, and also in letters 1 1/8" high with a nib of 1/16" wide. In these very heavy letters the constructive force and character of the pen are most obvious, but in the lighter ones they are not pronounced, & a greater call is clearly made of the writer's powers of drawing: it may also be seen that the lighter letters are susceptible of a greater variety in their width, & that they might, for example, be made half their width — without loss to their legibility. We may note particularly the remarkably different shapes inside, or "counters" as typefounders call them; the heavy letters showing sudden bends & angles compared with the smoother curves of the lighter letters. It may also be observed that these heavy letters incline to what is known as the "gothic" character, while the lighter incline to the "roman." These different effects will be discussed in connection

on on

3/8" letters, 1/8" nib   1 1/8" letters, 1/16" nib

with various different types a little later on.

It will be found helpful in practice to formulate a rough standard of weight, or rather, to associate our impressions of "heavy," "medium," & "light" letters with approximately corresponding ratios of width of thick strokes to height of letter. In penmanship it is convenient to use the nib of the pen itself as a measure and to express this ratio in nib-widths, which, with the pen held sideways, we may mark alongside the letter. Thus we may describe the heavy writing in the example on the following page as four nib-widths in height, or we may say that the ratio of its nib to its letter height is one-quarter.

The terms of weight here suggested for various ratios are, of course, purely approximate. But I imagine that the normal eye will agree very nearly with this, & also with the suggestion that generally a letter of a height below four-and-a-half nib-widths inclines to be heavy, while one above five-and-a-half nib-widths inclines to be light. I would suggest, further, that the "extra heavy" writing of three nib-widths high is about the heaviest writing that we may profitably use.

heavy ex.

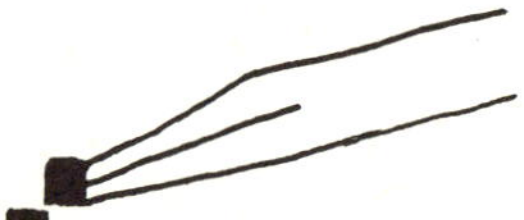

heavy

medium

light

Examples of letters of various weights of which the ratios are marked in nib-widths

(except, perhaps, in extraordinary cases;) & again, that we should not profitably use a much lighter writing (in ordinary cases) than the "light" writing of seven nib-widths. It is a good plan for the beginner to write rather heavily — say, with a ratio of 1 to 4, so that the pen will control his hand, &

it is also desirable that he should write large; very good proportions are half-inch writing with a pen of eighth-inch.

The normal range is roughly between four & six nib-widths high, but great variety is possible within this range, & it is to be observed, in the case of normal letter forms, that a comparatively slight difference in the relative height will make a considerable difference in the apparent weight of a letter, because ordinarily it involves a corresponding difference in the breadth. Thus a slight increase in height & breadth will make a considerable increase in the total area covered by a letter, and, as the penstrokes (remaining the same width) increase only a very little in their total length, it follows that the greater part of this increase in area will occur in the inside space of the letter (and, moreover, the adjacent spaces—outside the letter—will be affected proportionally). If we compare an n of four nib-widths with an n of five nib-widths, we find that, while the latter has an increase in height of only one quarter, & an increase

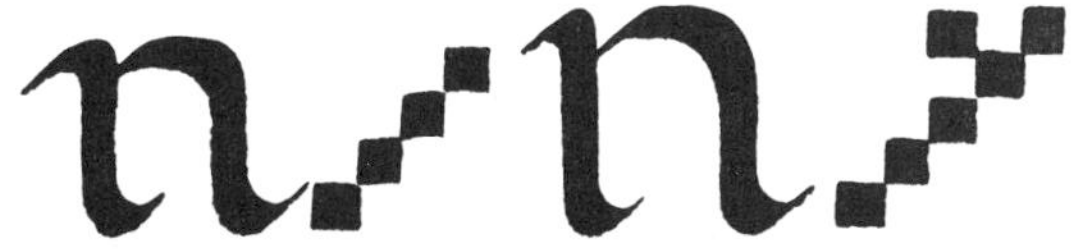

in the total length of its strokes of about one third, its internal space is nearly doubled; & it is obvious that this large increase adds greatly to the lightness of the letter. Such enlarged letters, in fact, may be said to be diluted or reduced in strength by the greater admixture of background.

While in practice their effects cannot well be separated, it will help to clear our conceptions of weight if we distinguish what may be called "actual weight" from what we may call "apparent" weight.

The "actual weight" of a writing, & of its letters, is best expressed by the weight of its strokes, &, as the vertical stroke (or direction of the stroke) largely predominates in our letters, we may call the letter i our standard for height & width. In this sense it will be found in practice that the actual weight may be very well expressed in the ratio of nib-width to height, as already suggested.

But that effect of weight, which may be distinguished as the "apparent weight," depends rather on the amount of its background, and is best expressed, inversely, by its spaces. In practice, we do not measure the letter's actual background, except by the eye, but occasionally it will be found to be of great value to measure in nib-widths the horizontal distance between the strokes. We may take the o as a standard. The internal space is of the greatest importance, but the proper background of an o is the whole of the internal & external space which belongs to it, & it may be approximately defined by a parallelogram described about the o:

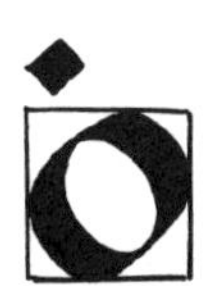

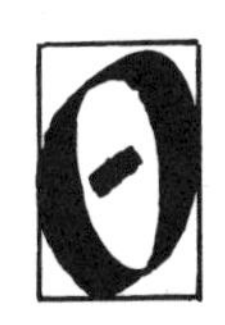

Various o's with their proper backgrounds

We may say, then that the "apparent weight," other things being equal, depends on the relation of the total area covered by the pen strokes, to the total area covered by both their internal & adjacent spaces. Generally speaking, a "light" letter has a comparatively large background, & a "heavy" letter has a comparatively small background: but as the vertical direction of stroke predominates in our letters, it is obvious that while the "actual weight" depends chiefly on the thickness of its strokes, "its apparent weight" depends chiefly on the distance between the strokes (or the number of strokes to a given space) that is to say, it depends on the breadth of the letters in relation to height.

The normal form of o is approximately circular; and the rest of the small letters follow it closely, being also approximately equal in height and in breadth. But there are also distinct narrow and wide types of letters, in which the o, together with the other letters, is compressed or expanded. If we contrast a normal & a compressed form we see how the two writings, written with the same pen & of the same height, differ in their apparent weights. Though this compressed writing has a much heavier effect, the "actual weight" of its letter forms is practically the same as that of the forms in the lighter writing: & as a number of narrow objects standing close together gives an effect of mass, so the apparent weight of the compressed writing is an effect of massing; rather than of actual massiveness. Nevertheless we observe, as a result of the compression, how completely the pen dominates the character

lighter writing compressed writing

of the example given, which, in practice, would be, properly, called a strong, if not a heavy writing.

Chapter II. The Development of Types, and Formal Writing: the Broad-Nibbed Pen—continued.

In considering the development of different types of letters, or characters, it is sufficient for our purpose to begin with the Roman capitals from which all our letters are descended. But a brief sketch of their supposed origin may serve, not only to show how natural & vital has been their growth, but to strengthen the hands of those who wish to preserve that fine tradition.

The invention of letters, or the development of alphabets from primitive forms or pictures has, for convenience, been divided into four stages which are called the Mnemonic, the Pictorial, the Ideographic, & the Phonetic. The signs used in the three later stages, representative of things, of ideas, & of sounds respectively, are called "Pictograms," "Ideograms," & "Phonograms." Among the primitive aids to memory, or Mnemonic symbols, Mr. Clodd refers to the knotted strings or Quipu of the ancient Peruvians, & the knot which we tie in our handerchief. Countless examples of these have been found both in the Old World and the New, & in both a similar, though probably an entirely independent, development appears to have taken place.

This remote & marvellous development we may faintly image thus: if, by a flight of imagination, we suppose ourselves to be primitive & without letters it is probable that our artists would, sooner or later, produce an approximate circle as a symbol or pictogram of the SUN. Then, in time, having become used to this & to kindred symbols and to purely pictorial records, we should go a step farther, & the circle might be made to stand for the ideograph of LIGHT. Finally – by a process resembling punning – the circle might come to be a phonogram for the sound Li or L, and we should at length have achieved a letter of the alphabet.

It may easily be seen how our apparently arbitrary Letter Forms are really economic simplifications of early pictograms: let us take two actual examples. In our letter M we can still discern the face of the OWL that was used by the Egyptians, in their hieroglyphic phonogram for M, thousands of years ago. In a monument assigned to about 4000 B.C. (preserved in the Ashmolean Museum at Oxford), the name of SEND is actually written alphabetically. We can even recognise the features of our own letter forms in these relatives.

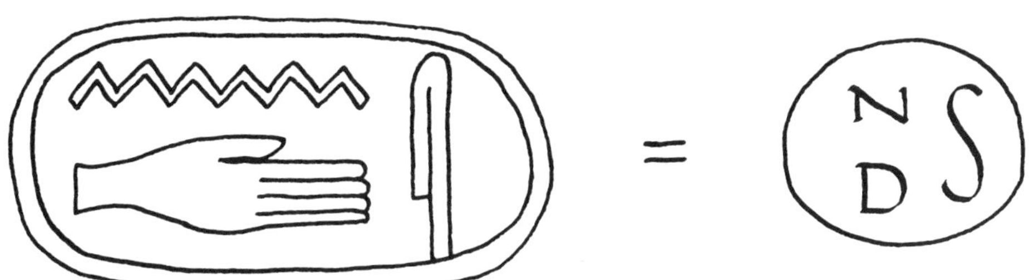

The earliest (Phonographic) writing extant, & its value.

Of the known ancestry of our own letters, that is of the ROMAN CAPITALS – an alphabet about 2500 years old – Sir Edward Maunde Thompson says, "The alphabet which we use at the present day . . . is directly derived from the Roman; the Roman, from a local form of the Greek; the Greek, from the Phoenician . . ." It had long been supposed that the Phoenician came from the Egyptian hieratic, but recent discoveries prove the existence, in very remote times, in all quarters of the Mediterranean & in Egypt, of symbols resembling certain alphabetical signs and preceding even the Egyptian hieroglyphics. The early origin of our alphabet therefore still remains to be worked out.

Judging from extant examples, the earliest Roman capitals were somewhat roughly formed & without thick & thin strokes. But the growth of the custom of cutting monumental inscriptions in stone led to a highly developed form in the first century B.C. These later inscriptions were carefully outlined or painted – commonly in red lead – before they were cut (and often painted in the same colour after). Such forms reached their highest development in the first & second centuries A.D. One of the finest examples is that of the inscription on the Trajan Column of about 114 A.D.

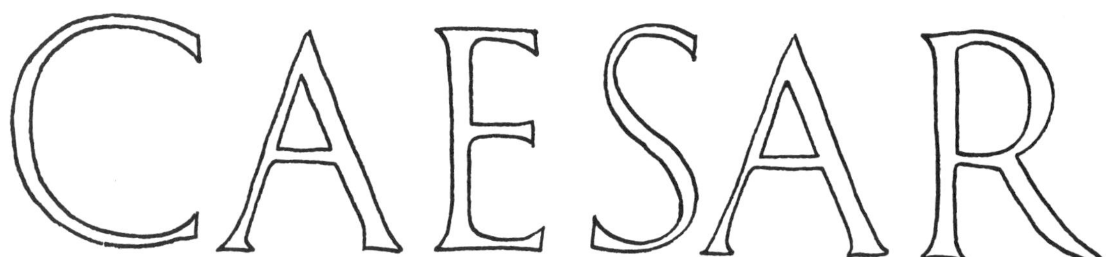

From the Trajan Column. SCALE: one-fourth of original

The cast of this (No. 1864-128) in the South Kensington Museum is worth studying. It will be seen that the strokes vary in thickness accordingly as they are vertical, horizontal, oblique, or curved, & that the curves are "tilted." Now, as this variety does not appear to come from anything in the stone & chisel themselves, or from methods peculiar to their use, we must look elsewhere for a cause. And as all these effects are necessarily produced by a broad-nibbed pen held at a natural slant, it is reasonable to suppose that the use of the pen may have strongly influenced the finished Roman characters. The careful carving in stone led no doubt to a formal type & possibly to the curving out of the stems, which, carried on into the serifs gave an effect of great elegance to the letter. An almost exaggerated example of this is given below (traced from Hubner's Exempla No. 149), a letter incised early in the first century A.D. But this earlier example also strongly supports

CAESAR

CAESAR

Characterisation of skeleton capitals by a broad-nibbed pen

the argument in favour of the pen's influence.

The letters of the earliest Latin Formal mss. naturally have a strong resemblance to the letters of the monumental inscriptions. They differ in this, that whereas the stone letters are built-up forms, the ms. letters are simple-written, & the varying widths of their strokes are in absolute relation to the breadth & the direction of the nib. It has been said in Chapter I (page 6) that the character of the broad-nibbed pen's writing depends partly on "the direction (or relation to a horizontal line) of the thin edge of the nib." In the next chapter this will be discussed further with the later ms. forms, but it well to realise at once the striking effects that changing the nib's direction produced in the development of types. Broadly speaking, we may hold the pen straight or slanting (a.b.); or what is more usual—we may alter the direction of the nib by cutting it at different angles to the shaft (c.d.). For many years I

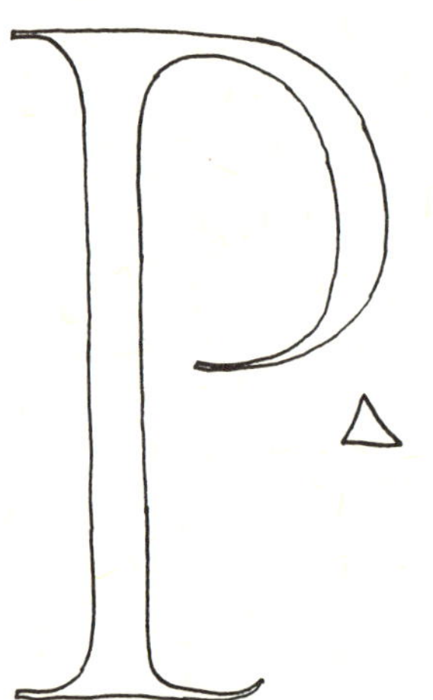

From Hubner's Exempla No. 149. SCALE: one-eighth original height

have called the mode of writing that produces a horizontal thin line, "straight-pen" writing, & the mode that produces an oblique thin line, "slanted pen" writing. Those these terms are convenient, when they are understood, I propose in future to

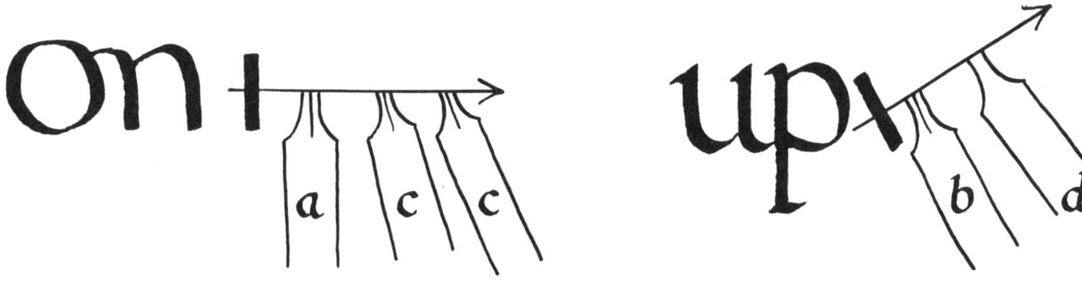

Straight-pen or Horizontal-nib *Slanted-pen or oblique nib*

use the more explicit terms "horizontal-nib" & "oblique-nib" writing.

The chief point to be observed in the effects of these two modes are the following: the horizontal-nib writing naturally produces a rather slow, round, formal, upright, & elegant letter, having a forward movement; the oblique-nib tends to produce a rather rapid, angular, compressed, heavy-shouldered, & strong letter, having an up & down movement.

In practice all formal writing shows the use of a more or less oblique-nib, though some of the most remarkable mss. show a thin stroke so nearly horizontal that we are justified in calling them horizontal-nib writings; indeed, if we attempt to copy these mss. we actually find it necessary to pretend that the nib is horizontal. The natural conclusion that it is easier to write with an oblique-nib may be immediately confirmed by a few minutes practice, & we shall find that it is borne out by the history of formal writing wherein both the primitive & the advanced stages are marked by its use.

The earliest, most formal, Latin mss. are assign-to about the fourth century; their letters are known as "Square Capitals" & "Rustic Capitals". In the former the obliqueness of the nib is rather less than in the latter; while, in both, the nib-direction is subject to considerable variation – which indicates

SQ. CAPITALS — R. CAPITALS

Square Capitals — Rustic Capitals

a slightly artificial, though quite legitimate mode Though writing of a less formal sort, in the style of the Rustic Capitals, is found in the earliest extant Latin mss. & of the earliest known mss. in

Square Capitals is ascribed to the end of the fourth century, yet there is reason to suppose that the square form (as it did in the stone inscriptions) possibly preceded the Rustic form. The latter, being written with a more slanted pen, may have been a more easily written pen development of the former. Books do not appear to have been written in either of these hands after the close of the fifth century, though the Square to some extent, most notably the Rustic, survived in ornamental titles, and the like, for many centuries. The survival of the Rustic may indeed be compared with the present survival of "black letter" for ornamental use: it is a testimony to the greater ease in writing it & to its ornamental qualities, which might justify the revival of the Rustic for occasional use.

Chapter III: The Development of Types, & Formal Writing with the Broad-Nibbed Pen—continued

IN the last Chapter, reference was made to our ancestral type—the Roman Capital—being about 2500 years old, & it was shown that about the beginning of the Christian era, inscriptional forms were fully developed and the formal ms. was merely a pen-made variety of the capital.

We must leave the pen for a moment & consider the effect on this development of another tool, i.e. the stylus. While a careful formal letter on papyrus (which became still more finished on the introduction of vellum) was used by the scribes for a book-hand (that is to say, for the making of books), the ordinary writing of the people consisted generally of skeleton capitals which were rapidly scratched by means of a metal or ivory

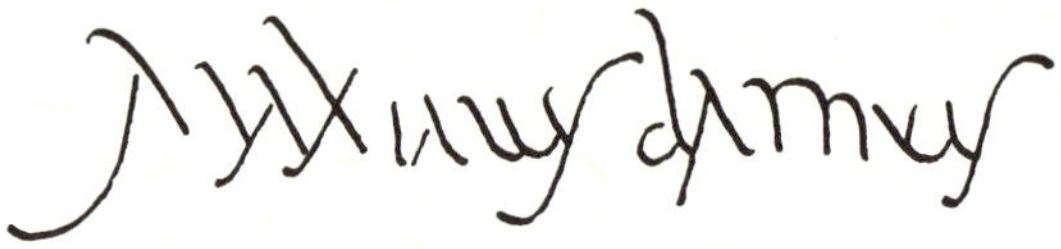

[MAXIMUS BATONIS]

Wax Tablet (Dacia) March 17th, 139 A.D.

stylus on wooden tablets coated with black wax. In this process the Roman Capitals inevitably underwent an economic development, having their strokes reduced in number or otherwise simplified, as shown opposite.

It is worth noting that two letters, at least (A&B) had two quite separate developments that eventually appear to have merged, in each case, in one

Capital	Development	Small letter
A		a a a
B		b
D		d
E		e
G		g g g
G		
H		h
R		r r
V		u

Centre shows development of Roman capital into small letters. Most of the forms were scratched with a stylus in the first & second centuries, but the last (lower) a (upper) b, d, (upper) g, r, and u are cursive pen forms of the 6th century. Forms in square brackets conjectural.

form (a & b), the two a forms, if they did not actually merge, were, at any rate, at one time very closely related. The forms in the second development of b are known to have existed, but as I have no facsimiles to copy them from I have put them in round brackets. The other forms are from Maunde Thompson. It is also to be noted that we can still trace the ancestral capitals in the features of our small letters and that there appears reason to suspect that the Roman capitals have always made their dominant influence felt. B and b, for instance, are most obviously related & yet by the first development of b the stem seems to have stood for the bows, and the bow for the stem, of its ancestor.

We see how greatly the stylus affected the development of our letters, &, though it made only ~ skeleton forms, its effects (coupled no doubt with the individuality of its users) were sufficiently remarkable to have given us the word "style" implying fashion) which is directly derived from it. Let us then, remember, in relation to Decoration, that any naturally handled tool will inevitably produce its natural or proper effects.

Chapter IV: The Development of Types, & Formal Writing with the Broad-Nibbed Pen — continued

THE development of types is here concluded by figures illustrating the letter forms used by the first printers. Such technical flaws as may be found in their books by a modern critic are far outweighed by the breadth of their conception and their simple magnificence, to which our blocks at secondhand do but scant justice.

The early printers have been accused of "imitating" the style of the ms. book. It is to be remembered that while we think of books as printed books, to the first printers & their public, books were written books — the work & traditional production of the penman. The normal attitude of mind towards any craft or art is worthy of attention: while our friends, for example, compliment us who are trying to revive the book-hands, or formal writings, by saying "How beautifully you print," doubtless it is by a corresponding confusion of thought that some antiquarians have been led to accuse the early printers of making imitation mss. The common processes of thought necessarily refer to

DERIVATIVES OF THE ROMAN LETTER

Derivative	*Name*	*Date of use*
From Greek	Roman Caps	c. 600 B.C. to present
(Stylus varieties)	Roman Cursive	-1st to ? 6th
(Pen varieties)	Roman Sq. Caps	(?-1st) to 5th[*]
	Roman Rustic	-1st to 5th[*]
From Capitals and Cursive (influenced by Greek Uncials?)	Roman Uncials	(2nd to 4th) 5th to 8th
From Cursive & Uncials	Rom. Half-uncials	5th to 6th
From Roman Half-uncials	Irish Half-uncials	7th to 8th[‡]
From Irish Half-uncials	English Half-unc.	c. 634 to 840[‖]
From Roman Cursive	Merovingian (Fr.)	7th to 9th
	Visigothic (Sp.)	(?-8th to 12th
	Lombardic (It.)	-9th to 13th

Derivative	Name	Date of use
From Merovingian Roman Half-uncial & English influence	Caroline reform (caroline or Carlovingian writing	c.-796 A.D. to 804+ †
From earlier native hands through Caroline reformed hands	Compressed angular hands of N. Europe	-12th to 15th
	Open (round) Italian hands	11th, 12th, and 15th §
From Compressed angular hands *(above)*	Black Letter or Gothic types	c. 1455 to the present day
From Italian Renaissance hands *(above)*	Roman small types	1501 to the present day

*Used later for special writing. ‡The Book of Kells ‖ Durham Book. † In France, at Tours, under Alcuin of York; established in England in the 10th century §15th century Italian hands directly modelled on native 11th & 12th century hands by Renaissance scribes the new in terms of the old, but, while ackowledging this necessity, we should endeavour to keep our minds clear & unconfused & receptive to the true nature of things. I cannot attempt to do justice to the overwhelming importance, especially to would-be decorators, of the question of what a thing is, but I shall recur to it at every opportunity & try to show that it is the first concern of every man.

The first printers' types were naturally & inevitably the more formalised, or materialised letters of the writer. The likeness of the type in the earliest book (the Mainz Psalter) to the French mss. of the fifteenth century is very clear.

We may now cast our eye over the first 2000 yrs. of our Roman letter's development: we find its beginning in a skeleton Alphabet (derived from Greek forms) & then occurs, on the one hand, a formal characterisation of this alphabet (carved or written by craftsmen) influenced & largely produced, by the broad-nibbed pen, & on the other hand, a less formal characterisation resulting from the scribbling of the educated public: this development at first controlled by the tool and

iustū: propterea egredit̄ iudiciū puer-
sum. Aspicite in gentibꝫ ⁊ videte ⁊ am-
miramini et obstupescite: quia opus
factū est in diebꝫ vestris: qd̄ nemo cre-
det cū narrabit̄. Quia ecce ego suscita-
bo chaldeos gentē amarā ⁊ velocem
ambulātem sup latitudinem terre: ut
possideat tabernacula nō sua. Horri-
bilis et terribilis est: ex semetipā iudici-
um et onus eiꝰ egrediet̄. Leuiores par-
dis equi eius: et velociores lupis ve-
spertinis: et diffundētur equites eiꝰ. E-
quites nāqꝫ eius de lōge venient: vo-
labūt quasi aquila festināns ad come-
dendū. Omnes ad p̄dam venient: fa-
cies eorꝫ ventꝰ urens. Et congregabit
quasi arenā captiuitatē: et ipse de regi-
bus triumphabit: et tyrāni ridiculi e-
ius erūt. Ipse sup omnem munitionē
ridebit: ⁊ cōportabit aggerē: et capiet
eā. Tūc mutabit̄ spiritus: ⁊ pertransibit
et corruet. Hec est fortitudo eius dei sui.
Nūquid nō tu a principio dn̄e deus

Portion of page of first printed book, 42-line Bible: 1450-1455

material, the stylus and wax tablets of the public, was mastered by them, the "scribblers", & became an economic development, simplified strokes & linkings or loopings, saving both time & space. The craftsmen in their turn, borrowing these more economic skeleton forms characterised them afresh by means of the broad-nib, and, in the mediaeval writings, achieved characters of unequalled clearness & beauty. Having reached this summit of perfection the professional tended to degenerate, the development of

Dñicis diebz post festũ trinitatis. Inuitatoriuum,

Regẽ magnũ dñm venite adoremus, ps Venite.
Dñicis diebz post festũ ephie Inuitatoriũ.

P venite aũ Seruite.

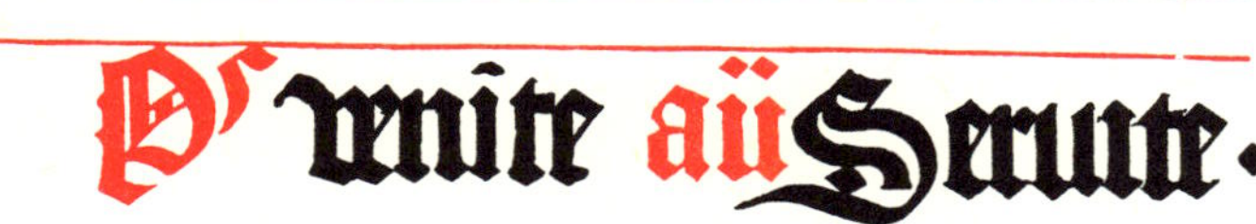

Eatus vir qui non abijt in consilio impiorũ et in via pccõꝝ nõ stetit: ⁊ in cathedra pestilẽcie nõ se=dit, Sed i lege dñi voluntas ei9: et in lege eius meditabit̃ die ac nocte. Et erit tanq̃ꝫ lignũ qđ plãtatũ iste

Euouae.

secus decursus aquaꝝ: qd fructū suū dabit in
tpe suo Et foliū ei⁹ nō defluet: ⁊ oīa quecūq
faciet ꝓsperabūt, Nō sic impij nō sic sed
tanq̄ pulvis quē ꝓicit ventus a facie terre,
Ideo non resurgēt impij in iudicio: neq
peccatores in cōsilio iustoꝝ Quō novit dūs
viā iustoꝝ: ⁊ iter impioꝝ peribit, Gl'ia P

First page of the Mainz Psalter of 1457 printed by Fust and Schoeffer. It has been reproduced by woodcutting from the original copy on vellum in the King's Library of the British Museum

Mainz Psalter, 1457

formal writing becoming firstly economic, by a more rapid style & by compression & reduction, and, secondly, ornamental, by an over developmt of the details of form, & the combination of writing with ornament,— that is familiarly known as illumination. At the critical moment, the early printers appeared on the scene, & the importance of the letter form & of readableness again became predominant. It is interesting to note in passing how each nation played its part. The Romans, who obtained their alphabet from the Greeks, passed on their best hands to Ireland; the Irish, perfecting these, passed them on to England, & the English hand is thought to have influenced the reformed hands in France. The French gave these

to in alcuna coſſa haueſſe p ignorātia o per inaduertentia manchato trāſformato: ouer incompoſitamente pferto ueramente rechiedo perdono ſempre ſopponendoui ad ogni ſpirituale & temporale correctione de qualunque diuotiſſima perſona di zaſchaduno perito maeſtro & ſapientiſſio doctore de la uoſtra ſāctiſſima madre eccleſia catholica di roma.

ANNO A CHRISTI INCARNATIONE. MCCCCLXI. PER MAGISTRVM NICOLAVM IENSON HOC OPVS QVOD PVELLARVM DECOR DICITVR FELICITER IMPRESSVM EST.

LAVS DEO.

Venice, Jenson, 1471; Colophon Decor Puellarum, *misdated 1461*

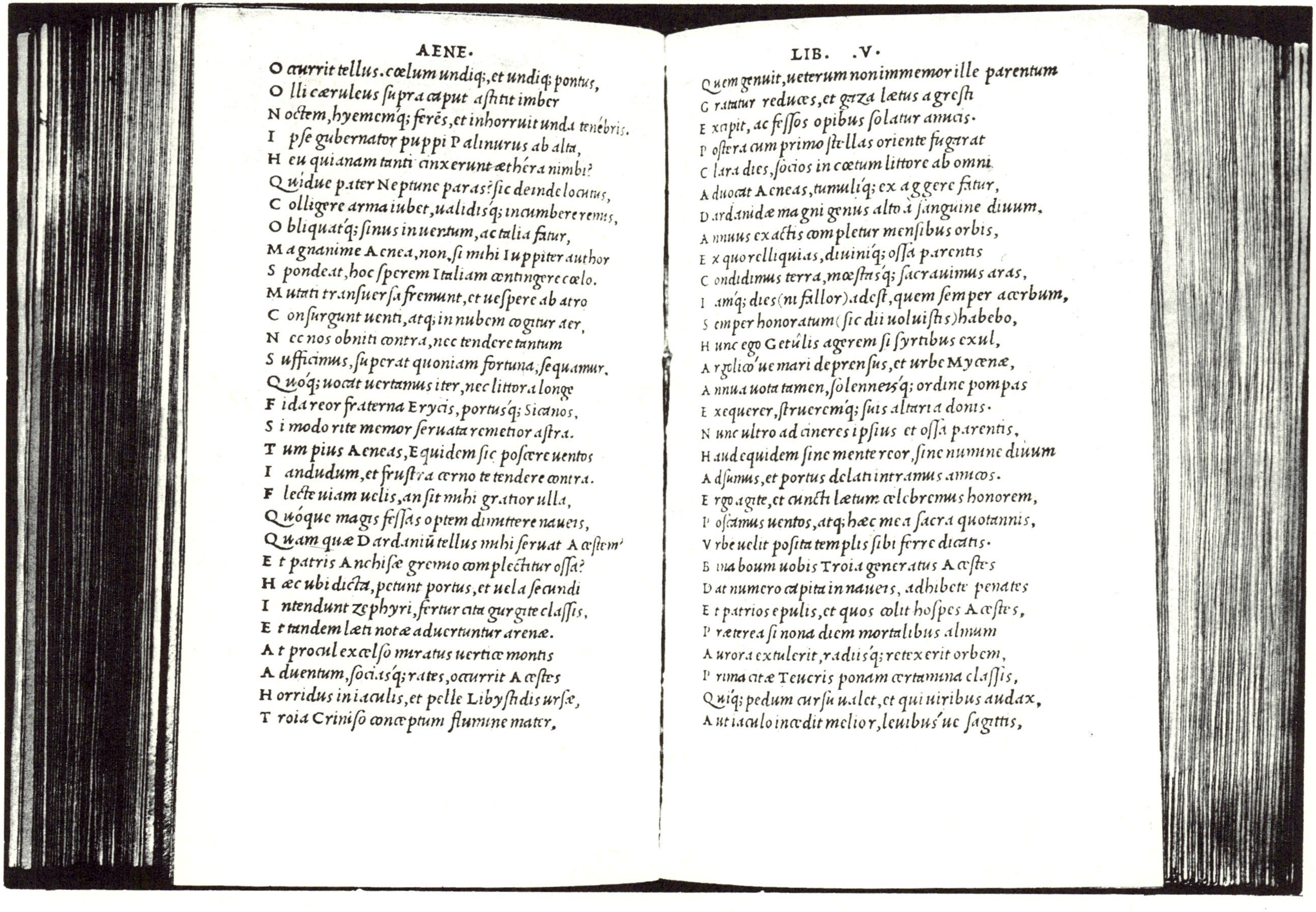

O ccurrit tellus. cœlum undiq;, et undiq; pontus,
O lli cæruleus supra caput astitit imber
N octem, hyememq; ferēs, et inhorruit unda tenebris.
I pse gubernator puppi Palinurus ab alta,
H eu quianam tanti cinxerunt æthera nimbi?
Q uidue pater Neptune paras? sic deinde locutus,
C olligere arma iubet, ualidisq; incumbere remis,
O bliquatq; sinus in uentum, ac talia fatur,
M agnanime Aenea, non, si mihi Iuppiter author
S pondeat, hoc sperem Italiam contingere cœlo.
M utati transuersa fremunt, et uespere ab atro
C onsurgunt uenti, atq; in nubem cogitur aer,
N ec nos obniti contra, nec tendere tantum
S ufficimus, superat quoniam fortuna, sequamur.
Q uoq; uocat uertamus iter, nec littora longe
F ida reor fraterna Erycis, portusq; Sicanos,
S i modo rite memor seruata remetior astra.
T um pius Aeneas, Equidem sic poscere uentos
I andudum, et frustra cerno te tendere contra.
F lecte uiam uelis, an sit mihi gratior ulla,
Q uoque magis fessas optem dimittere naueis,
Q uam quæ Dardaniū tellus mihi seruat Acestem?
E t patris Anchisæ gremio complectitur ossa?
H æc ubi dicta, petunt portus, et uela secundi
I ntendunt zephyri, fertur cita gurgite classis,
E t tandem læti notæ aduertuntur arenæ.
A t procul excelso miratus uertice montis
A duentum, sociasq; rates, occurrit Acestes
H orridus in iaculis, et pelle Libystidis ursæ,
T roia Criniso conceptum flumine mater,

Q uem genuit, ueterum non immemor ille parentum
G ratatur reduces, et gaza lætus agresti
E xcipit, ac fessos opibus solatur amicis.
P ostera cum primo stellas oriente fugarat
C lara dies, socios in cœtum littore ab omni
A duocat Aeneas, tumuliq; ex aggere fatur,
D ardanidæ magni genus alto à sanguine diuum,
A nnuus exactis completur mensibus orbis,
E x quo relliquias, diuiniq; ossa parentis
C ondidimus terra, mœstasq; sacrauimus aras,
I amq; dies (ni fallor) adest, quem semper acerbum,
S emper honoratum (sic dii uoluistis) habebo,
H unc ego Getulis agerem si syrtibus exul,
A rgolico'ue mari deprensus, et urbe Mycenæ,
A nnua uota tamen, solenneisq; ordine pompas
E xequerer, strueremq; suis altaria donis.
N unc ultro ad cineres ipsius et ossa parentis,
H aud equidem sine mente reor, sine numine diuum
A dsumus, et portus delati intramus amicos.
E rgo agite, et cuncti lætum celebremus honorem,
P oscamus uentos, atq; hæc mea sacra quotannis,
V rbe uelit posita templis sibi ferre dicatis.
B ina boum uobis Troia generatus Acestes
D at numero capita in naueis, adhibete penates
E t patrios epulis, et quos colit hospes Acestes,
P ræterea si nona diem mortalibus almum
A urora extulerit, radiisq; retexerit orbem,
P rima citæ Teucris ponam certamina classis,
Q uiq; pedum cursu ualet, et qui uiribus audax,
A ut iaculo incedit melior, leuibus'ue sagittis,

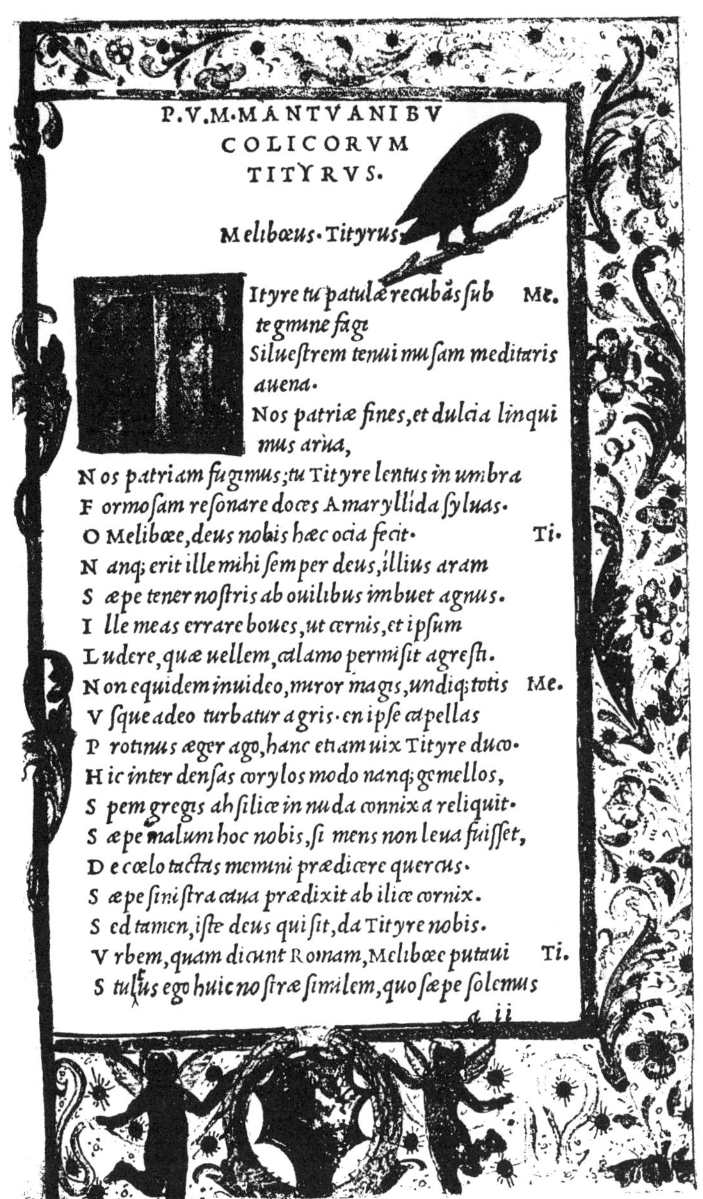

P.V.M.MANTVANI BV
COLICORVM
TITYRVS.

Melibœus· Tityrus

Ityre tu patulæ recubãs ſub Me.
tegmine fagi
Silueſtrem tenui muſam meditaris
auena·
Nos patriæ fines, et dulcia linqui
mus arua,
Nos patriam fugimus; tu Tityre lentus in umbra
Formoſam reſonare doces Amaryllida ſyluas·
O Melibœe, deus nobis hæc ocia fecit· Ti·
Nanq; erit ille mihi ſemper deus, illius aram
Sæpe tener noſtris ab ouilibus imbuet agnus.
Ille meas errare boues, ut cernis, et ipſum
Ludere, quæ uellem, calamo permiſit agreſti.
Non equidem inuideo, miror magis, undiq; totis Me.
Vſque adeo turbatur agris· en ipſe capellas
Protinus æger ago, hanc etiam uix Tityre duco·
Hic inter denſas corylos modo nanq; gemellos,
Spem gregis ah ſilice in nuda connixa reliquit·
Sæpe malum hoc nobis, ſi mens non leua fuiſſet,
De cœlo tactas memini prædicere quercus·
Sæpe ſiniſtra caua prædixit ab ilice cornix.
Sed tamen, iſte deus qui ſit, da Tityre nobis.
Vrbem, quam dicunt Romam, Melibœe putaui Ti.
Stultus ego huic noſtræ ſimilem, quo ſæpe ſolemus
a ii

Venice, Aldus, 1501. Virgil in Italic letter

hands to the rest of Europe, and the Italians finally gave the world the small roman and italic forms. The first printers were Germans. I have dwelt on this matter because we see in brief in the development of types how very natural was their growth: a growth more natural in writing than in any other craft — if we may call any thing more natural than another — because, in its essence, it was more subservient to its purpose, more rapid, & less thought out. A well-known designer once said "You scribes are the fellows, you don't have to think at all." This is true in its best sense, & the first lesson I would draw from penmanship, for the consideration of decorators, is that natural growth should take the first place in their work, for conscious design is only tolerable when it is the act of one thus set free, of one to whom the right thing comes naturally because his work has grown naturally.

Chapter V: The Choice of Letter Forms and the Simple Arrangement of Letters: Formal Writing with the Broad-Nibbed Pen—continued

INSTINCTIVE choice is the decorator's soundest guide: if it be encouraged it will bring us thro' all the theories unscathed—even those that we ourselves create. But our instincts have been so much disused or abused that Reason must be called to our aid. How many, in these days, who are interested in decoration know what they really like? It is no passing fancy or doubtful attraction, but it is that which we really like that matters & that ought to triumph at last over all materialistic systems & rules. Let us then honestly try to find out what we really like, &, in the meantime, endeavour to be reasonable.

Now if we are to choose letter forms, the only reasonable course open to us is to do so on the basis of readableness. We will, however, make our basis as wide as possible; we therefore take readableness to imply not only easy-to-read but also pleasant-to-read. If, for the sake of clearness, we here distinguish these qualities, we may also say that, while it is the general function of the craftsman to make a thing legible, it is his particular function as a decorator to make it becoming. We have found then that one of the Uses of Decoration is to make a thing pleasant to read; but, unless the decorator – like the poet – is "born," he must begin at the beginning and deal first with the more practical side of readableness, that is, with legibility.

There are three things which constitute legibility, namely simplicity, distinctiveness, and proportion. Besides these abstract qualities there are various concrete aspects of legibility: the two most important are accustomedness & fitness. We do not require new forms in this sense, "that which is new is not true"—but, though we must accept the symbols of present use. Our current letters—whether of printing, or of common writing, or however made—are the Roman Capital, the Roman small letter, & the italic; & it is with these three forms that we must ordinarily deal, regarding ornamental & others as departures from the standard, and therefore as marked for occasional use. Fitness, i.e. the suitability or adaptableness for a given purpose, will be considered in connection with special cases. The broad-nibbed will create for us a standard of its own, not a departure from the current standard, but a variety, just as printer's types—though they seem nearly to fill the whole field of vision—are themselves a variety (or varieties). I give here a reasonably representative version of this pen standard. The pen standard, which with a little care we can all of us recreate, has the peculiar virtue—as far as the small letters are concerned—of being essentially the ancestral type (so that, literally, all other varieties are varieties of it). The example of it is given here in the hope that decorators may

ABCDEFGHIJKLMNOPQRSTUVWXYZ skeltns

PEN: ABCDHIJMOR

abcdefghijklmnopqrstuvwxyz "roman" small letter skeletons

pen·abcdfghijklmoqrstuv

xyz "rom". foundational hand

abcdefghijklmnopqrstuvwxyz italic skeletons

pen·abcdefghijklmoqrstuvwxyz

Skeletons of the current standard forms & a suggested Pen standard (in oblique-nib writing). Note: The natural pen hooks and strokes are here used for terminals (serifs)

acquire it, or a similar formal hand. Having such at our command, we may experiment purely in form & arrangement of letters, & it is certain that most of us can in this way discover the "theory & practice" of decoration more easily and more surely than by any other means.

Simple written Roman Capitals. It will be remembered that certain early mss. were written entirely in capitals, but when the new manner of writing in small letters came into use it was regarded as *a different writing*, complete in itself. The Roman Capital survived in the shape of important initials & in headings, etc., but we do not find it written to match the small letter writing of the mediaeval mss. Nevertheless we can make it for ourselves by using the same pen, held in the same manner, as we use for the small letters. For example, the capitals in the last illustration are simply what the pen makes of the ordinary abstract or skeleton forms. Similarly – among the various forms of the Roman Capital – we can take *round* (or "branch-topped") and *flourished* capitals and characterise them with the pen.

Roman small letters. The ms. example shown on page 43 is made from the skeleton small letters which are given there; but, in effect, it is almost identical with the ancestral 10th century ms. By using a narrower nib, & by making stroke terminals, a still more "Roman" hand can be made from this as shown opposite.

BDDEFH M PRTUW Round or Branch Topped Romans

BDDEFHMPRTUW

AABBDDEEFFGHILMMNRRTVW Flourished Romans

AABBEEFGILMRT

"Branch-topped" & Flourished Roman capitals with a pen

Italics. The ms. example on page 43, though based on the skeleton italic which is given there, is derived directly from the foundational hand above it (by compression, elongation of *ascenders & descenders*, & slight sloping). It can also be made more "Roman" by the use of a narrower nib.

It is to be observed that from this pen standard small letter on page 43, which I call the "founda-

abcdefghijklmnpqrstuvx

A more "Roman" development from the pen standard or the "foundational" hand

tional" hand, various more "Roman" forms may be derived, & also various italic forms; & we will find that, by using a broader nib, we can also make of it a more "Gothic" character, and can so develop a "black letter" variety.

heavier and more "gothic" & "black-letter" development

Besides being useful in itself, particularly as an educational hand, its forms therefore an excellent general basis for further development & I would strongly recommend its acquisition by craftsmen generally. It may be noted here, that, other things being equal, the open hands are more legible than the compressed, & the forms of medium weight are more legible than the heavier forms. The most legible hand will probably be found to have an externally circular o, and a stroke-weight of about one-fifth of its height.

For the general "qualities of good writing" I shall at present refer the reader to the section & the table, under that name, in my handbook. But the three abstract qualities referred to as constituting legibility may be graphically illustrated here:

I. Simplicity: that is, *having only necessary parts.*

II. Distinction: that is, *having marked features.*

III. Proportion: that is, *having each part of its proper value.*

I have in the following example designedly chosen a quite passable (modern) black-letter capital, as a foil, to illustrate in the abstract the nature of legibility. If it were desirable for this purpose to exhibit "horrid examples" how many of our ordinary "display" types could be refused a dishonourable place? Perfect legibility is not always necessary &, occasionally, even undesirable: but a departure from the legible standard requires a reason or, in other words, a compensation, to justify it. For example, the value of a black-letter (both capital & small letter) as an occasional form, is largely due to the fact that, without an increase in "actual weight", it will give an increase in "apparent weight", by which we may obtain a vivid contrast with our Roman type.

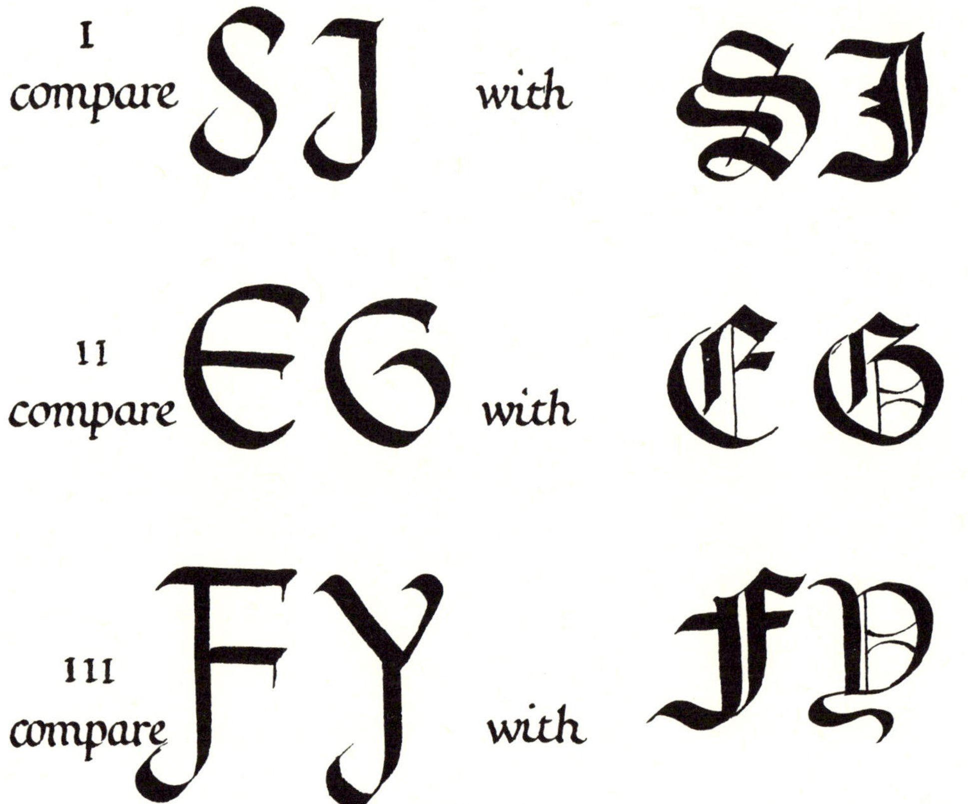

Contrast of more and less simple, distinctive and proportionate forms

We can thus state in a general way the qualities & features that should be sought when we aim at ordinary legibility, & for general purposes the "foundational" & related hand given fulfil the conditions. But for special purposes, we make (or, more correctly, the circumstances themselves make) special developments which give the particular quality of fitness.

For those who wish to take up formal writing more thoroughly, a course of practise in the "straight-nib" forms helps to form the hand (& I think the judgement too). The simplified "half-uncial" hand below is very good for this purpose. The characteristic difference between this and

+ abcdefg ABCDEFG

Modern half-uncial

the foundational hand will be appreciated best by practical experiment: reference may be made to the comparison of "straight-nib" writing with "oblique-nib" writing on page

Using our standard hands as "counters" we can now proceed to the question of the Simple Arrangement of Letters. It will be found that all the previous remarks on readableness of form apply equally to arrangement: so that legibility also requires a Simple / Distinct / Proportionate / Familiar & Fitting } Arrangement.

The familiar arrangement of letters is the placing of a number of lines in a rectangular space. But we can simplify our conceptions of arrangement if we put the matter thus:

In general, treatment of lettering is the treatment of LINES of letters. Therefore, in general, the line is a much more important unit than the page.

Among the phenomena of familiarity we may note that by use our eye is trained to accept the vertical rules of newspaper columns in lieu of margins, so that we generally remain blind to the contents of the neighbouring columns. Fitness of arrangement, as before mentioned, is the development for (or, more properly, by) some special use.

Chapter VI. Special Arrangement of Letters—the Book: Formal Writing—continued

THE reiterated statement of the last chapter must again be quoted: "Fitness (of form or arrangement) is the development for (or, more properly, by) some special use." A special use implies a special object or Thing. Now I must ask the reader's patience if – attempting a task which is as greatly difficult as it is supremely important – I labour the point of this.

If we intend to make some Thing, the clearest conception possible of *what that thing is* is our first concern; for that which it is in deed is the realisation of our intention. I say the clearest conception possible, because it is doubtful if a man can be quite clear as to what he intends until he has done his work; but to achieve reality it is essential that we have a measure of clearness in our intention.

It may be said of a man working vaguely, that, setting out to make a chair, he finds that he has made a table, by mistake. This accident is not peculiar to *carpenters*, indeed carpenters are less prone to it than most people, because their stuffs & their tools so often carry them through. Perhaps we may hazard the guess that the *artist* & the *legislator* vie with each other in producing the greatest number of accidental effects; but

but no man is free of this fault, for in fact every man is an artist & a legislator; let him deny it with his tongue if he please.

Strictly speaking, human success is a happy accident: but that half-god Luck – whom we think so well of that it is common to wish a man "good bye & good luck" (Good b'ye seemingly having lost its original meaning) – that luck, so vitally helpful as it is, so strangely unaccountable, may at times not only lead us but be persuaded to follow; for if we ourselves follow right ways, happy accidents become a habit. The right way to set about making a chair is to intend "chair" with all our will; our old friends simplicity, distinctiveness, proportion, come to our aid, and if we are happy, the chair – legible, or at least recognisable – will be achieved.

I think it will be admitted that clearness of intention, though related to definiteness bears a finer sense, as of something made visible and shining rather than something limited & outlined. And it is desirable to point out that such clearness of intention do not necessitate great planning or scheming, & that overplanning is one of the greatest dangers we have to beware of. Its speciousness misleads the practical: it is far worse than under-planning — the "chair" of the mere dreamer may be passable, but the chair (or sofa) of the schemer, we have been told, was convertible into a table or a step-ladder. Thus the schemer achieves confusion, & over-reaching himself, falls into much deeper error than the witless. This applies alike to the humblest works & to the greatest; between a chair and a cathedral there is only a difference of degree, the table & the tavern are relations; the "workman" whose "chair," by lack of meaning, becomes a "table", or the "architect", whose "cathedral" becomes a "tavern," does less harm than the schemer whose "cathedral" will have a *barber's shop* and a *crematorium (& shops on the ground floor to pay the rent.*

The objection to overplanning applies to all pre-designing – which, in its tendency to suppress natural growth in the working, forms the almost unsuperable difficulty of the professional "designer" who is not a craftsman, & is the acknowledged solicitude of all good architects who are not builders. The remedy is to know what we are aiming at and, at the same time, to allow our work to grow naturally. This apparent paradox is not self-contradictory, as the work of the early craftsmen proves for us, & as we, in our work, may prove again. Man's general aim in respect of his work may be hinted at — *to do his work well* is probably near the mark. Beauty — in its finest sense perhaps the ultimate aim — is more truly a divine reward than his direct objective. Thus I would attempt to plead with decorators who desire something finer than the riot of "display" decoration — as we may call it — of the modern world, to seek for simplicity in their intentions together with clearness; then, if our methods are right, the work will grow by nature beautiful.

What then are right methods? Here is the practical problem of every man's craft. We can only speak generally — natural growth implies natural & workmanlike methods, that is to say, the methods of tradition or the methods developed by the work itself. In the treatment of special examples I shall endeavour to show, as far as possible, in these papers, how these methods may be followed, & how proper methods may be resolved.

For our first example we will take the book – a subject which I can only introduce in this chapter, & hope, in the next, to develop in some detail. The book, as we know it, consists of a number of leaves hinged together at one side. Its treatment differs from that of the broadside or panel inscription (which is like a single page) chiefly in this, that the several pages of the book being numerous and – inasmuch as they are bound at one side & free at the other – not symmetrical, we may take as many pages as we want, not having to fit our text to one given page, but continually turning over a new leaf, & we also treat the several pages, in relation to their binding, symmetrically. Symmetry of text & margin is, of course, the general rule in the "opening" of the book, that is, in its opposite pages taken together. The book is *portable* & therefore it is not so dependent on its surroundings as a panel or wall-inscription is.

The approximate proportions & arrangement of the opening of a mediæval book are shown on the following page.

Chapter VII: Special Arrangement of Letters — the Book (continued). Formal Writing with the Broad-Nibbed Pen — continued.

It is now to be shown in the making of a ms. book, the exemplar of the printed book, how "natural and workmanlike methods" are followed & are "developed by the work itself."

The first considerations are the nature & use of the book: these demand a suitable treatment of its subject matter & an accustomed & fitting shape for its purpose. Its treatment therefore

2

Manuscript commonly occupying less than a half of the page-area

3 1½ 3

is so placed thereupon as to allow of margins thus varied in width 1½ 2 3 4

4 4

follows tradition & custom, insofar as they are natural & healthy, rather than extravagant design.

Generally the size of the book is first settled; that is, the size & shape of its leaves are determined approximately. And though, in deciding whether a book shall be "large" or "small" or of a medium size, we are naturally influenced by the subject matter; *use* is the chief guide; & it is such things as these that the right craftsman bears in mind, whether it is

to lie on a desk or be carried in the pocket,
to lie on a table or be held in the hand,
to be used often or seldom,
to be "useful" or "ornamental."

A large subject will stand being written "large," but it will also stand being written "small." A small subject on the other hand, must seek a modest medium—written large it becomes immediately ridiculous. The student will find it stimulating to make books decidedly "large" or "small": the necessities & opportunities of the case are then most apparent, and indeed go so far to fulfil themselves. Thus it is more easy to make a great book grand or a little book pretty than it is to give interest of form to a medium-sized book.

It is proper to let the actual proportions of the leaf be finally decided by the shapes & sizes into which our ordinary skin of vellum or sheet of paper may be naturally cut or folded. We may, however, take such a skin or sheet as will give us something near our approximate choice. It is known that the sizes of sheets of paper are traditional, & that a sheet folded once gives us a *folio*, folded once again a *quarto*, & folded a third time an *octavo*, so that we know, for example, that the page of a "Royal" quarto is one quarter (in area of a "Royal" sheet. But possibly it is not so well known that, in spite of the number & variety of the traditional sheets, the ratio of *length to breadth* in every case approximates to the ratio of 9:7. Therefore whatever the size, the proportions of the leaf of the book – that is, of its height to breadth – are approximately regular, being in the case of folio & 8vo. as 7:4½, & in 4to. & 16mo. as 9:7.

It is a good plan to regard these as our regular proportions for leaves, only departing from them when we have a special reason and an opportunity for so doing.

Generally the next thing to be settled is the size (& proportions) of the margins. In ordinary printed books the total area given to margins is about half the area of the page—that is, an equal area to that of the text column. The margins are generally greater or less than this accordingly

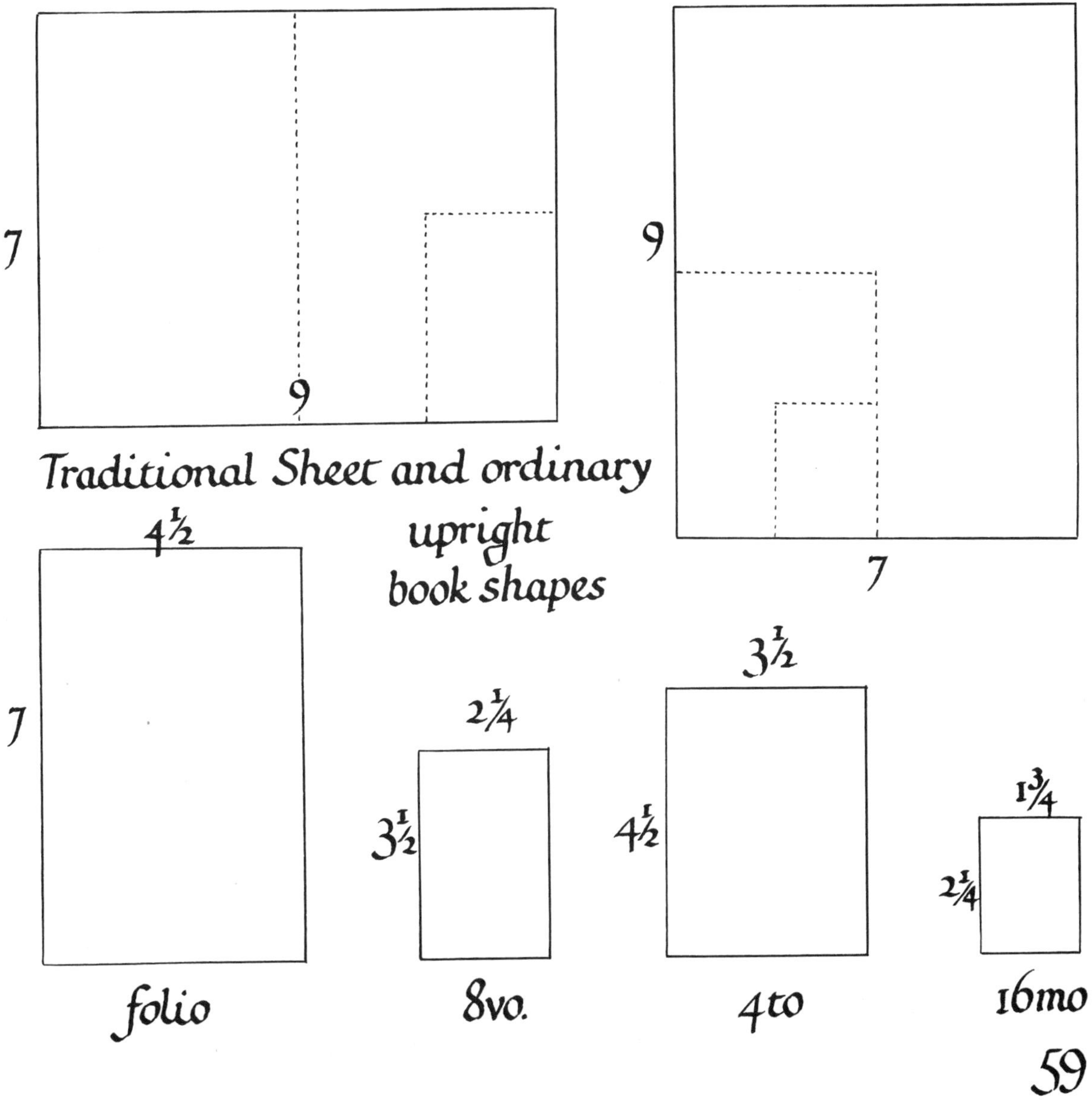

Traditional Sheet and ordinary upright book shapes

as the books are better class or cheaper productions; though very small books, e.g. prayer books, even when fairly well produced, commonly have smaller margins for the sake of economy. All things considered there is no one thing that is greatly at fault in ordinary books, but the modern printer (or publisher) is too apt to be lavish of wide margins without rhyme or reason in fancy publications, while he is almost criminally economical of them in cheap editions.

The purpose of the margins is chiefly to make the text more readable by isolating or framing it: they are therefore essential to the normal book which is held in the hand & comparatively near the eye. Other books (such as desk books (where they are not so necessary still follow the fashion of the normal book.

In the case of a ms. book we cannot do better than follow the ancient fashion as our normal rule. The margins of the mediaeval ms. commonly comprised more than half (say three-fifths or more) of the page area. The names of them are shown on one page & their ratios on the other; in the figure on the opposite page.

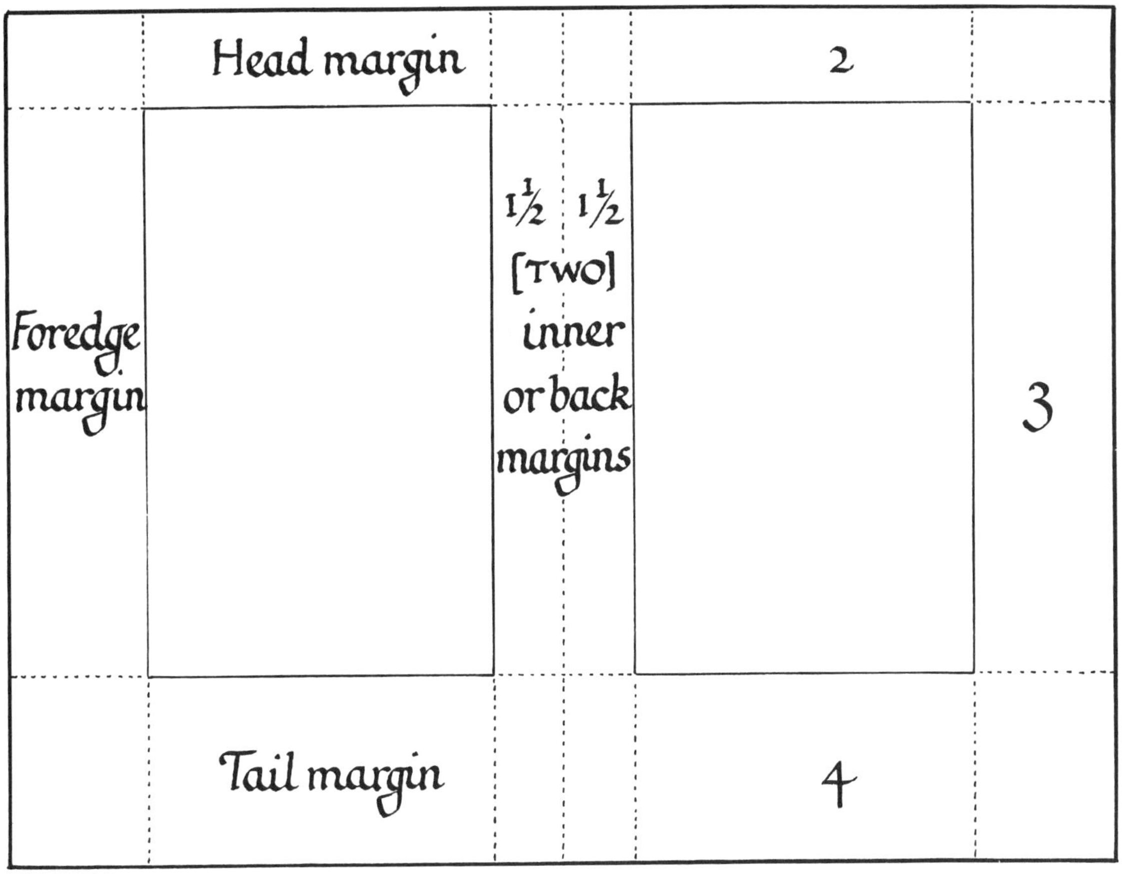

Head margin 2

Foredge margin

1½ 1½
[TWO]
inner
or back
margins

3

Tail margin 4

This fashion was the outcome of natural growth & use, and was the custom among people who valued books in a way that we can scarcely realise. We may therefore feel sure that it wasn't a case of "art-nonsense"—as "wide margins" and most of the trappings of the so-called "Decorative book-work" of the present day are apt to be.

We may attempt to explain the mediaeval margins thus. The previous statement that the margins are essential to a book will be generally admitted, & it will be seen that as the reader's eye is focussed on the page & is running forward and back along the lines of text, it adds greatly to his comfort if a wide foredge margin intercepts his eye from falling ("over the edge" at it were) on the floor or walls or on any other object of a varied texture *on a near but different plane*. The notably wide foredge margin of the mediaeval book does therefore add greatly to the reader's comfort and pleasure, in short, to the readableness of the book. It was the custom to make the two inner margins *together* approximately equal to the foredge margins. This breadth, although not so necessary as in the foredge margins, allowed for the loss of width that is apt to occur through the bending of the leaves at the middle fold. If we consider the two narrow inner margins — as they always come together — as forming one broad one (thus $1\frac{1}{2} + 1\frac{1}{2} = 3$), it will be seen that the head margin is in effect the narrowest in the book, & we may reasonably suppose that the eye running horizontally & having once read the headline, required no further margin there. The deep tail, sometimes very deep, was evidently allowed for a hand-hold & to prevent thumbing of the text. Its most important aspect, that of *the space which is left* (after the page has been written will be dealt with in the general discussion of margins.

Should anyone have difficulty in setting out margins, I offer the following formula for the common folio or octavo proportion of leaf, namely, 7 : 4½: make Height of Text column equal the Width of Page; make Width of Text column two-fifths of the Height of Page.

The area of text will then equal two-fifths of the page area, and this will allow the correct proportions, 1½ : 2 : 3 : about 4½.

Having then, a given page & margins, we are left with a given space to fill with text; we have therefore to settle the treatment of *the line of writing*. The length of this line is already determined, so that our main concern is with the size of the letter. If there is no special consideration in favour of a special size of letter, we take that size of letter which will give us a convenient number of words to a line. The ordinary book has, speaking roughly, from 8 to 10 words in the line: to have much more than this or to have much less is very tiresome to read. The student who at first will not be able to "pack" his words tightly may try about six words. The average English word, with its succeeding space, takes about five letter-spaces; for a six-word line about 32 letter-spaces will be required. If, then, for example, our given writing line be 8", this would allow 32 letter-spaces of ¼" each. Roughly we may reckon the normal letter-space to be a *square*, therefore in normal letters our 8", six-word line will take ¼" writing.

We have still to settle the distance between the lines. It is best to allow too much space here than too little, but the normal course to follow is to allow the *ascenders* and *descenders* just to clear each other. Thus, if we put a p over a d, this will give us our line space which, if fully spaced will be about three times the height of the o, as illustrated. In the case of normal ¼" letters fully spaced, this will be 3/4". Our line-space thus given we find how often it will go into the height of the given text space, & thus we get the number of lines to the page. Slight compromises are made in the fitting all together, as, for example, if there is some little space over we may throw it into the tail.

Thus we may see in the matter of size & shape of the book, of its margins, & of its writing and spacing how the work itself develops methods & how the broad outlines of the plan are, in a sense, settled for us. To permit this phenomenon is one of the first steps, and perhaps it is the last, in the "practice" of Design. Doubtless to some, these things may all seem obvious, & there would indeed be no use in recapitulating them were it not for the gross or perverse misapprehension of elementary methods that is a feature of this Advanced Age. The present writer does not claim to be entirely exempt.

Example of normal letters fully spaced

THIS BOOK WAS WRITTEN BY ME, JOHN CHARLES TARR, IN LONDON AND FINISHED ON THE FIFTEENTH DAY OF DECEMBER IN THE YEAR 1930

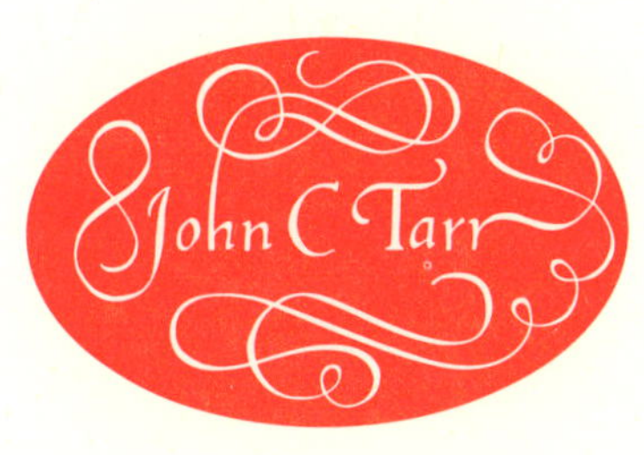